M000166221

THE
CAPRICORN
ORACLE

THE
CAPRICORN
ORACLE

INSTANT ANSWERS FROM
YOUR COSMIC SELF

STELLA FONTAINE

greenfinch

Introduction

Welcome to your zodiac oracle, carefully crafted especially for you Capricorn, and brimming with the wisdom of the universe.

Is there a tricky-to-answer question niggling at you and you need an answer?

Whenever you're unsure whether to say 'yes' or 'no', whether to go back or to carry on, whether to trust or to turn away, make some time for a personal session with your very own oracle. Drawing on your astrological profile, your zodiac oracle will guide you in understanding, interpreting and answering those burning questions that life throws your way. Discovering your true path will become an enlightening journey of self-actualization.

Humans have long cast their eyes heavenwards to seek answers from the universe. For millennia the sun, moon and stars have been our constant companions as they repeat their paths and patterns across the skies. We continue to turn to the cosmos for guidance, trusting in the deep and abiding wisdom of the universe as we strive for fulfilment, truth and understanding.

The most basic and familiar aspect of astrology draws on the twelve signs of the zodiac, each connected to a unique constellation as well as its own particular colours, numbers and characteristics. These twelve familiar signs are also known as the sun signs: Aries, Taurus, Gemini, Cancer, Leo, Virgo, Libra, Scorpio, Sagittarius, Capricorn, Aquarius and Pisces.

Aries Taurus Gemini Cancer Leo Virgo

Libra Scorpio Sagittarius Capricorn Aquarius Pisces

Each sign is associated with an element (fire, air, earth or water), and also carries a particular quality: cardinal (action-takers), fixed (steady and constant) and mutable (changeable and transformational). Beginning to understand these complex combinations, and to recognize the layered influences they bring to bear on your life, will unlock your own potential for personal insight, self-awareness and discovery.

In our data-flooded lives, now more than ever it can be difficult to know where to turn for guidance and advice. With your astrology oracle always by your side, navigating life's twists and turns will become a smoother, more mindful process. Harness the prescience of the stars and tune in to the resonance of your sun sign with this wisdom-packed guide that will lead you to greater self-knowledge and deeper confidence in the decisions you are making. Of course, not all questions are created equal; your unique character, your circumstances and the issues with which you find yourself confronted all add up to a conundrum unlike any other... but with your question in mind and your zodiac oracle in your hand, you're already halfway to the answer.

Capricorn

DECEMBER 22 TO JANUARY 19

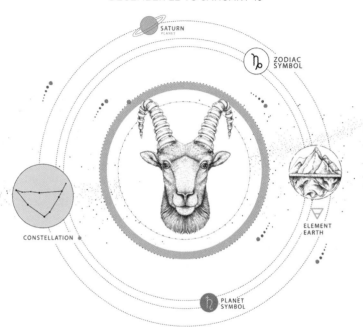

Element: Earth

Quality: Cardinal

Named for the constellation: Capricornus (the horned goat)

Ruled by: Saturn

Opposite: Cancer

Characterized by: Discipline, strength, self-control

Colours: Brown, black

How to Use This Book

You can engage with your oracle whenever you need to but, for best results, create an atmosphere of calm and quiet, somewhere you will not be disturbed, making a place for yourself and your question to take priority. Whether this is a particular physical area you turn to in times of contemplation, or whether you need to fence off a dedicated space within yourself during your busy day, that all depends on you and your circumstances. Whichever you choose, it is essential that you actively put other thoughts and distractions to one side in order to concentrate upon the question you wish to answer.

Find a comfortable position, cradle this book lightly in your hands, close your eyes, centre yourself. Focus on the question you wish to ask. Set your intention gently and mindfully towards your desire to answer this question, to the exclusion of all other thoughts and mind-chatter. Allow all else to float softly away, as you remain quiet and still, gently watching the shape and form of the question you wish to address. Gently deepen and slow your breathing.

Tune in to the ancient resonance of your star sign, the vibrations of your surroundings, the beat of your heart and the flow of life and the universe moving in and around you. You are one with the universe.

Now simply press the book between your palms as you clearly and distinctly ask your question (whether aloud or in your head), then open it at any page. Open your eyes. Your advice will be revealed.

Read it carefully. Take your time turning this wisdom over in your mind, allowing your thoughts to surround it, to absorb it, flow with it, then to linger and settle where they will.

Remember, your oracle will not provide anything as blunt and brutal as a completely literal answer. That is not its role. Rather, you will be gently guided towards the truth you seek through your own consciousness, experience and understanding. And as a result, you will grow, learn and flourish.

Let's begin.

Close your eyes.

Hold the question you want
answered clearly in your mind.

Open your oracle to any page to
reveal your cosmic insight.

Mixing business with pleasure,
or home with work, is standard for you
Capricorn. With boundaries already
blurred, it is essential you clearly
demarcate some time and
space just for you.

Resist your Capricorn urge to focus so intently on the finish line that tunnel vision obscures everything else along the way. There is much to be learned during the journey.

No one can fault your
analytical Capricorn approach,
but perhaps (just perhaps) it might
not always be essential to see the
immediate risk versus benefit balance
sheet for every decision. Try stepping
back on this one, to see the
bigger picture.

Of course, not every sign
is as precise and thorough as you,
Capricorn, and that's why they get it
wrong more often than you do. But
once in a while you need to loosen up
and trust that the universe might bring
you exactly what you need, as
long as you just relax.

Are you so determined to control how everyone else sees you that you might be letting an opportunity pass you by? Worth considering...

Driven by lofty ideals and a
deep-seated desire to scale heights,
the mountain goat in you loves a
challenge. Embrace this side of
yourself; it is about to give you
a distinct advantage.

Patience and persistence
will be key to your success.

Do not invest that which you
cannot afford to lose, and keep your
own counsel Capricorn. Your wisdom
and clarity of thought is strong
– allow it to guide you.

When you know what it is
you really want, there is nothing more
powerful than that ruthless logic
Capricorn is so famous for.

Take a day off. (That means
a holiday by the way, not a day to
catch up on all the work you can't get
done when you're actually working.)

You are pure goat – stubborn
and tenacious, every step of the way.
And that's no bad thing. It pays off
usually... But some things work better
if you let them come to you.

Even valuable insights can be confusing out of context. It's important to be absolutely clear about what you know.

Try saying 'yes'.
Something different might happen.

When a little distance is required Capricorn, you should prioritize attending to your own business, pull back a little, and find your own way through. The right thing will land with you soon enough.

There are plenty of potential excuses, but also many opportunities just waiting for you... don't miss out on them. In reality, perceived obstacles are often nothing of the sort.

It is vitally important you are honest with everyone involved in this issue. Self-knowledge is never a weakness and allowing yourself to be truly seen takes particular courage.

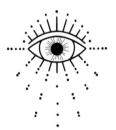

Yes, we know, you're not 'negative' you're realistic. But bear in mind that too much focus on the risk and danger lying in wait all around could maybe, possibly, perhaps stop you reaching your full potential.

The decision to do what is right is not always the easiest path to follow. But it is your path.

Your stars have gifted you with
remarkable powers of perception –
don't cloud the matter by focusing on
your preferred outcome. Allow all
and any, then see what comes.

You love to know what's going on, understand the problem, explain the thing. But not everyone is looking for The Answer.

A sequence of small wins
is the secret to true success.

You have only to live your own life, no one else's. Stop seeking to make comparisons Capricorn, it is a senseless waste of your brainpower, your energy and your time.

Your typical Capricorn impulse
is to stay the course and maintain that
hard line until you get results. Simple
as that. But there is nothing more to
be gained with this one, holding on
longer than anyone else will
just drag you down.

Creativity and imagination
might not be skills you score yourself
highly for. But remember: these gifts
come in many guises.

Deep immersion in your
work is admirable, of course, and
a big part of what makes you proud
to be you. But it can also provide the
perfect excuse for isolating yourself;
when you are inside that fortress and
pull up the drawbridge, no one can
touch you. Don't be tempted to
avoid your real life.

Celebrate your victories
Capricorn, and not just the big
ones. Small steps are milestones along
the way, and just as significant
– do not disregard them.

Persisting with pushing ahead,
to the exclusion of all else, is not
necessarily the only way to reach
the solution that is right for you.

Make your own plans and
resist the temptation to be swayed
by others. Copying someone else
won't get you very far (but by all
means watch what they are
doing and learn from it).

Capricorn self-discipline is second-to-none, that goes without saying. But is it always necessary to make the sacrifice? Sometimes, the universe wants you to have the reward regardless. Enjoy it.

Home is your haven, and that makes perfect sense. But sorting through your wardrobe or the 'useful things' cupboard for the umpteenth time still might not guarantee that the world outside falls into line. Something to think about.

Resist the urge to focus down
too far; all this meticulous planning is
admirable, of course, but getting it
done is what actually matters.

Intention or action?
It's time to make your decision.
(Psssst: these are not mutually
exclusive.)

Stick to your route Capricorn;
it's your nature to map out the
simplest and most straightforward
plan, and that's the one you
should follow now.

Wilful, determined,
driven and perhaps even a little
stubborn... sound like anyone you
know Capricorn? Take a break from
striving for perfection to make things
flow more smoothly for yourself and
those around you, too.

You might need some help
dealing with this problem Capricorn;
different opinions and input will
benefit the solving process and
ensure nothing is missed.

Resolving this one depends
on finding the middle ground and
rooting yourself firmly there – it is
where you are most comfortable after
all. Biting off more than you can chew
would be a mistake right now.

You are naturally risk-averse,
Capricorn, even though you know
that sometimes risk is necessary when
you want to aim for those big rewards.
If you find yourself asking, 'Why wasn't
I braver?' a little too frequently, think
about ways you could engage with
more courage.

You love getting to grips with things Capricorn, especially if it involves making a detailed plan using a spreadsheet or a list or, if your stars are really lining up, maybe both. Teasing all these knotty bits apart and then laying them out cleanly and neatly will bring you extreme satisfaction – don't let anyone take that away from you. Do your thing.

Of course, you are a serious
person with lots of important
decisions to make. But now might be
one of those rare and precious times
you should just throw caution to the
wind and treat yourself to what
you fancy. And maybe another
one after that.

Work hard, work hard – that's your motto. But take the time to see what lies off in the distance today; you need some perspective on this one.

Check in thoroughly and honestly with yourself, to be sure you are not sacrificing too much. Is this taking too great a toll on your physical, emotional or mental health... or perhaps all three? If not, fantastic. If yes, you will need to prioritize where to best spend your efforts.

Grounded and pragmatic?
Naturally; you're the earthiest of Earth
signs! But try reaching for the stars
with this one – you have so much
potential and you just might
surprise yourself.

The Capricorn goat sometimes presents as a sea goat; never forget this secret duality in your nature. Take a tip from your fish-tail and move smoothly around any obstacles like water flowing around a stone.

Don't be too hasty to rush into an exciting-looking venture Capricorn... make sure you read the small print carefully first and allow yourself a decent cooling-off period before you properly commit.

Show yourself some love
Capricorn – anything is possible.
Try approaching this one from a
different angle, or looking at it
through a different lens.

Do not be persuaded into
action by jealousy or envy; make
the best decisions you are able to for
yourself, rather than trying to emulate
someone else's choices or lifestyle.

You are so capable Capricorn,
that it's sometimes hard to imagine
there might be anything you can't do
all by yourself. But try to accept some
help this time – it may make things
that little bit easier.

Relinquishing control can feel risky, especially when you know others tend to take a more 'relaxed' approach, shall we say... But going with the flow does not necessarily equate to drifting.

Forgive yourself for your mistakes.

Prioritizing emotion over strategy at the moment will infuse your life with sudden clarity and direction. There may even be surprising changes you feel compelled to make – don't over-think things, just go with your heart.

Remember that taking care of yourself means nourishing your mind, body and soul. If you can find a way to combine the three, you'll be satisfying your heart's desire for efficiency as well!

With Cancer as your opposite sign, sometimes you need to give your ever-practical working mind a break and trust your intuition. Now is one of those times.

The answer will be right in
front of you, as long as you are asking
the right question.

Deeply compassionate,
Capricorns can sometimes be read
as cold or calculating by those who fail
to understand your need to protect
your own vulnerabilities. This
judgement says more about them
than it does about you; do not
concern yourself with the
opinions of others.

Trying to cope alone will create a burden heavier than you actually need to carry. Ask for help with this one. You may be surprised at how warmly your request is received.

Structure and certainty are fine, if they're your sort of thing (and they really are Capricorn...). But don't shut down all possibility of spontaneity – good things often lie on the other side of that predictability wall.

Actions speak louder than words; you are what you do, not what you say.

Take a detour from your usual determined problem-solving style this time Capricorn; work around the immediate issue, modify your expectations and (tough as you might find it) adopt a more flexible approach.

Thinking for yourself is a significant Capricorn strength; maintain your personal clarity and focus now.

Self-doubt is a slippery slope Capricorn. You must commit to a course of action.

If you feel the urge to mix things up a bit, to add in some excitement, you should act on that. Changing your approach will bring a freshness and a freedom you have been craving, something often missing from the Capricorn routine. Don't concern yourself with what others might think – their reactions will be their own responsibility.

Your true friend is the one
who tells you what you need to hear,
not just what you want to hear.

Congratulate yourself on
how far you have come, rather than
focusing on how much further
there is to go.

Set aside your impulse
to head-butt your way towards
what you think you want and
instead wait to see what the
tides might wash your way.
You know they will turn.
They always do.

Overcoming obstacles is a particular skill of yours, whether you find a way around or just plough straight through. That talent will serve you well now.

Of course, we all love to hear positive things about ourselves, Capricorns perhaps more than most (even though you pretend it doesn't affect you at all). Resist the urge to be led by flattery.

Becoming frustrated with a repetitive routine? Help yourself out by making a move in an out-of-the-ordinary direction; say 'yes' to something you would usually refuse or initiate an interaction you would normally avoid.

Take the risk of making a fool of yourself Capricorn. Breaking away from your ego's control is vital if you are to stand a chance of real success.

On this occasion, your growth
may very well depend on doing the
thing you are most afraid of.

Listen to yourself Capricorn.
It may be time to regroup and
recalibrate; do not fight what your
body, mind and soul are telling you
they need right now.

Take a break from transmitting
and learn how to listen.

One of the wisest signs there is,
Capricorns are never deluded into
thinking that life is supposed to be fair.
Fun? Sometimes, perhaps. Fair? No.
That is the root of your tremendous
work ethic; it will not fail you here.

Usually you are so clear-headed;
resist the urge to pick an option
while your emotions are in
the driving seat.

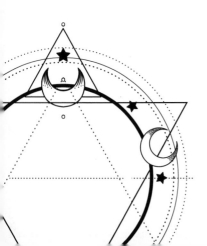

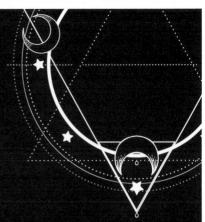

It may be that adversity brings opportunity, or it may simply be that you are having a bad day. You don't need to figure it all out right away.

Yes, you can.

But it doesn't mean that you should.

Don't undersell yourself,
no matter your audience. You
know your own worth Capricorn, even
though you are not necessarily one for
shouting it from the clifftops. Remain
steadfast, secure in your
self-knowledge.

Pick a direction, don't sit on
the fence or linger in the doorway.
Life is too short for dithering.

It's never too late for an
apology, whether from you or to you.
Remember Capricorn, sometimes
even you might get things wrong.

Your tremendous work ethic and deeply committed nature can lead some more 'opportunistic' signs to look for ways to exploit you... they will only make this mistake once. Adopt a clean, straightforward approach to butting this one firmly out of the way before things go too far. Leave no room for doubt. Then move on.

Make the little things count;
they keep you company more often
than the big things, and they
will shape your days.

Try as you might, you cannot rewrite the past. But your future is entirely in your own hands.

Think carefully about
whether someone from your
past might have something to bring
you, ask of you or offer you at the
moment Capricorn. Even if there is no
transaction to be done, listen carefully
to your heart and think about
getting in touch again.

The answer is right in front of you;
do the thing you won't regret later on.

Mature and responsible, you
are also determinedly individualistic,
in true Capricorn style. But your
careful approach might mean you
miss out on an opportunity now
and then. Take a chance.

You are brave and driven Capricorn;
persevere and you will get there.

Follow your urge to discover
and explore Capricorn; there is so
much you still need to experience,
and to learn.

Headstrong, like the goat you are, you can be toughened in your thoughts and set in your ways. Yes, you. Really. Loosen up a bit on this one and see what happens.

Dealing with adversity is one of your super-skills Capricorn, and, given your propensity for planning, often actually brings you opportunity. Help others to see past the immediate issue to get through this. You don't need to plan more than a few steps ahead at a time – save the big-picture thinking for later.

Patience is certainly one of
your star-given Capricorn virtues;
you have an unusual gift for
persistence. Bear in mind, none of
the other signs have been gifted with
quite the same endurance levels, and
they might find staying the course
without some rewards along the way
less satisfying than you do.

Accepting that you may be enduring a situation imposed by someone else can be a struggle. Resentment will quickly rise to the top if you are not careful Capricorn. Allow that sometimes this is just how it is and maintain a steadfast approach without engaging or actively opposing more than you have to.

Resist your conservative Capricorn urge to close down your options; allow them all, and the right one will make itself known soon enough.

It is more effective to allow
than to force. Of course, you know the
best way already. But others might
take a little more time to realize...
patience is required.

Eliminating uncertainty is easier said than done Capricorn. But remember you don't need to be perfect. This decision needn't be flawless. Make your choice and start moving. You can adjust as you need to along the way.

Don't be too suspicious of an
easy win this time; something much
more difficult is just around
the corner.

Some might call you controlling
(the very idea...), but all you want
to do is protect your own hard work
and investment. Be careful your
cautious Capricorn instinct for comfort
and security doesn't tip over into
something else.

Prioritize your loved ones and nurture your relationships, rather than allowing your attention to be distracted by what looks like an easy win. Pretty as it looks, it may turn out to be nothing more than a fantasy.

Find a way to carry on.
Slowing your pace at this point will
not guarantee the best rewards.

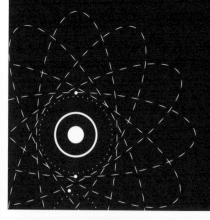

The key to tackling this unwieldy issue will be to allow rather than to block... Agree first, keep the conversation and momentum flowing, go along with it. This is the most positive way to find the right direction.

Ambitious and hard-working
with a nose for success – that's all
classic Capricorn. But don't forget that
softer, more vulnerable part: the you in
you, which is the bit that
really matters.

There is a chance you are over-thinking this; just be careful your (unnecessary) attempts at correcting self-consciousness won't be misinterpreted as indifference.

Sometimes you have to allow
the risk of being hurt in order to
give yourself a real chance of
something else. Being too cowardly
to try at all is the real failure.

Your stars have blessed you
with so many unique talents, and
great intelligence. Don't hide your
light; make sure those around you can
benefit from your wisdom as well.

Take things slowly now; it is more in line with your cautious Capricorn nature. You will know when the time is right.

It is time to look ahead and focus on the future. Your talents for positivity and leadership will be in great demand.

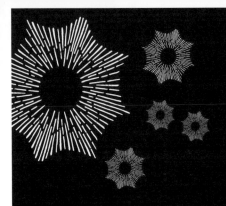

You have accomplished some
great things; pause for a moment to
reflect on them with pride.

Allow yourself to be inspired
by your surroundings Capricorn,
no matter how mundane they may
seem at first glance. There is fresh
learning to be had in every situation,
whether you are inspired by external
factors, or soothed enough to allow
yourself to relax and turn inwards.

The concept of being swept thoughtlessly along with the crowd doesn't sit easily with you Capricorn. Your future is in your hands.

What you do is what you are.
If you have dreams and plans for the
future, for things you might do and for
the person you might become, now is
the time to make a start.

Switch on that Capricorn
self-discipline, pull yourself together
from the core and engage with
structure, clarity and intention.
Stand tall.

You will need your full measure
of Capricorn courage for this one.
Try to speak from your place of truth
rather than from a desire to receive a
response. Only then are you
ready to say something.

Don't get stuck in a pattern of second-guessing yourself Capricorn. Make a decision, then make your move.

Scaling what looks to others
like an impossible-to-conquer cliff
face will be pure simplicity for you
Capricorn. Your sure-footed, goatish
agility will see you safely to the top.

Keep your ego in check Capricorn;
letting it rule is a mistake, as you run
the risk of it taking over and throwing
a dampening blanket down on all the
lovely sparky bits along the way.
Aim for balance.

In your dealings with others,
hold back from headstrong or
hasty actions. Do not forget or
disregard their feelings; if you
do, your careful approach
may begin to unravel.

Messy situations are not within your comfort zone Capricorn – you feel much easier and less frazzled when everything is calm and ordered. Some signs thrive in chaos. You are not one of those signs.

Clarity and vitality go hand-in-hand for you Capricorn; it is hard to focus clearly when your energy levels are low. Remember to devote the time you need to maintenance, and nourish those around you as well; they will hold you up when you need it.

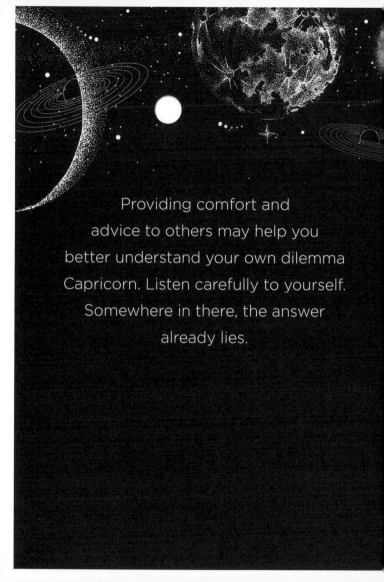

Providing comfort and
advice to others may help you
better understand your own dilemma
Capricorn. Listen carefully to yourself.
Somewhere in there, the answer
already lies.

Make up your mind, then stick
with it. Have the courage of your
convictions, and back yourself
to do the right thing.

Self-motivated and independent
as Capricorns can be, it's often hard
to remember that your choices have
an inevitable knock-on effect for those
around you. Consider likely outcomes
before you travel too far down a
path you might not be able
to reverse out of.

Pick your battles carefully
Capricorn and guard your energy
reserves for what lies ahead.

It is important to keep everything in order so you can lay your hands on what you need at a moment's notice Capricorn; it helps you maintain that direct and unfussy approach you are so well known for. Has someone else made a change you didn't know about? Asking questions is the only way to get to the bottom of this.

Setting high goals and working
hard to achieve them is admirable
Capricorn, no one would argue with
that. But take some time to consider
whether this wheel of striving and
attaining, striving and attaining is
really bringing you the peace
you truly seek.

To achieve your desired
outcome in good time, you will
need to be assertive and move others
along with you. Although you may feel
uncertain about pushing them, they
will thank you for taking the initiative.
If you wait too long, you may
all miss your the opportunity.

Your interest in understanding
others may well pay off right now.
A friendship or relationship you have
nurtured (read: scheduled some time
for) may reward you with some
fresh shoots and possibilities.

Don't allow resentment in if,
once in a while, you feel you haven't
received *quite* the acknowledgement
you deserve. You have done brilliantly,
and that knowledge will need to
suffice for now. Offer it up, let it go.

You're not exactly a thrill-seeker
Capricorn, but you don't shy away
from excitement (when it presents
itself in a manner that makes sense to
you). You definitely say 'yes' to the fun,
but you want to be part of controlling
how it happens. Try a different way
this time – go with the flow and see
what happens.

You have very few options
here Capricorn, but, luckily for
you, making a sacrifice should deliver
the reward. And there is no sign quite
as dedicated to sacrificing now to
secure a win later. In many ways, this is
your perfect puzzle – you were
made to solve it.

Opening that door to painful memories or difficult decisions you usually try to avoid is even trickier for you than for most. But it must be done and – gently, slowly, with a compassion you would normally not spend on yourself – you will do it.

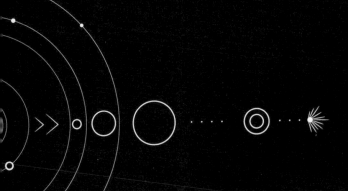

You must keep moving forwards Capricorn, the very fact you are considering this question means, at some level, that your curiosity is growing and perhaps you are no longer quite so afraid of the next step... If you need a distraction, music will prove a loyal companion.

Energy is all to a Capricorn,
and when you feel it running low
it's essential that you slow your pace
a little. More thought, less
haste right now.

You're efficient without even trying sometimes Capricorn, and often find yourself super-productive without too much effort or planning, almost as though it's your natural state... Now is one of those times; you might even surprise yourself!

Pause the rushing from have-to-do
to have-to-do and take a break from
all those terribly important tasks. You
may find, when you pause and look
around, that the thing you have been
working so hard for has already
been achieved.

Find inspiration in tackling things from a different angle Capricorn; your usual process, while familiar, might not be the only (or perhaps even the best) way to go about this. Take a less goatish approach this time. Use new information gathered along the way to make some improvements.

Conserve your energy and
take some time to turn inwards
– pushing outwards all the time
will not be possible if you don't
replenish yourself.

Set ego aside right now
Capricorn, doing things differently
needn't alter your sense of self. Quite
the opposite in fact – it will enrich your
perspective, enhance your
understanding and strengthen the
bonds of your relationships with
those around you.

Stop, look and listen. Valuable advice
for you Capricorn – whether crossing
the road or trying to still your busy
mind. Events are already in motion;
there is nothing you need to do.

Staying in place and allowing
the world to carry on can be
surprisingly difficult for you Capricorn
– but it is a valuable skill to learn. You
will notice much more if you simply
still yourself, watch and notice, than
you ever will in rushing.
Soak it all up.

Controlling Capricorns have
a difficult time with this kind of
problem or decision. It is important
to make peace with this truth: not
everything in life is manageable
through sheer determination and force
of will. Some things just happen.

It is time to devote some serious energy to achieving a sustainable balance between the different parts of your life; each must support the others in order for harmony to resonate. Otherwise you run the risk of losing something that matters very much to you.

You may sense that others are finding it difficult to understand your decision. If it is important to you, be sure that the way you are communicating your reasons is clear. If their opinion really isn't that important to you, don't bother.

Take some time to do as little
as humanly possible... not just
physically, but mentally too. Switching
off, or at least distracting yourself with
some satisfying and mindless tasks,
will open the door to a whole new
possibility you have previously
been missing.

Your work and responsibilities
take up so much of your time
Capricorn, you might be finding it
difficult to differentiate between work
and home. This isn't the first time you
have faced this issue, but things are
different now. Look for a fresh solution
and give some thought to
the spaces in between.

If the feeling that something is not
quite right is bothering you, perhaps
you should ask for what you need,
loudly and clearly, without leaving any
room for misunderstanding. Say it
as it is, or you stand no chance
at all of fixing this.

Feedback is not always required;
right now, it's best to bite your tongue.
Mindful listening is a rare and valuable
skill, and practice makes perfect.

Precious lessons from the past should inform your next move; knowing what you now know, you will regain control and find an effective solution much more easily this time.

Your reputation for keen intelligence and pragmatism is well deserved, and it combines with your strongly analytical approach... you love a challenge, and friends often approach you for advice. Be sure that you bring the same level of dedication to puzzling out the solutions to your own problems.

Your extremely strategic Capricorn style means that rarely, if ever, does anything escape you. You must be aware though that holding yourself in a constant pattern of high-alert will take a significant toll on your wellbeing. To keep everything in good working order, it is essential that you allow yourself a break from the adrenaline every now and then.

Avoiding or exiting difficult situations rather than sorting them out can be a Capricorn trait, and one you should correct. A half-done task is as bad as a task never even begun. Worse, in fact, if others think you are on top of it, but you are really leaving it to fester.

You goats have a reputation
for being stubborn and reluctant when
it comes to taking advice or trying a
different way. Go with the flow a bit
more; if something isn't working, look
for an alternative route.

Your Capricorn self-confidence means you are often sure you know best. But open your mind and bring some clarity and creativity to this if you can; others work differently and they may well have knowledge or information you could usefully employ. Don't be too stubborn to even give it a try.

Go with your instinct to let
your head rule over your heart
on this occasion Capricorn. Make the
decision clean and logical, precise
and easy to follow.

Sow the seeds Capricorn, then nourish and protect them. Give them some time and see what grows.

Your persistent focus pushes
this question to the front, but are
you sure there isn't really another,
bigger question you would prefer
to answer? Set stubbornness aside
and ask again.

The situation is not quite as it first appeared, and the circumstances are more complicated than perhaps you had assumed; picking your way through this looks like it could take a while. Time to put that famous Capricorn doggedness to work.

If your thinking is clouded,
or you feel less grounded than usual,
take advantage of this altered state
rather than being frustrated by it.
Usually so practical, Capricorn, this is a
chance to let some more intuitive
responses surface for an airing.

Relax your ready-for-a-fight stance
and take this opportunity instead to
listen to what the other person needs
to tell you. It might not be about the
issue you first thought.

Taking offence and absenting
yourself is not the solution Capricorn,
it is just a cowardly escape. Set
your ego aside and try to engage
wholeheartedly instead of looking
for a way out.

As you know Capricorn, delivering an unvarnished truth is not always the best way to endear yourself to the recipient. Counsel others to suspend their judgements, and, if they must have their say, to consider all likely outcomes first.

A wise and worthwhile friend will tell you what you need to hear, rather than simply stroking your ego. Or perhaps you would prefer silence Capricorn, but that is not an option. Loyalty and truth go together on this one.

Spending time with a number
of different people is preferable at
the moment Capricorn; too much
intensity or deep-and-meaningful at
this time might prove overly
draining. Keep it light.

Your process-loving approach
means that you occasionally run
the risk of missing some of the good
bits Capricorn. Taking pleasure in duty
and diligence is admirable, but there
are many other pleasures to be
enjoyed as well.

A strong vein of focus and concentration runs firmly through you single-minded Capricorns and gives you great pleasure – work is not all work to you. Your resourcefulness is a great gift, keeping you primed and prepared for almost all eventualities... just the way you like it.

Hold your tongue for now. It is
better not to have your say just yet
– in fact, you should wait until much
more of this plays out before you even
consider wading in. Perhaps by then
you will have changed your mind and
be able to simply leave it alone.

What you are currently feeling might not be all about your current circumstances Capricorn; your subconscious has a way of blowing a secret dog-whistle every now and again to alert you to the fact that there are underlying issues.

You love a plan Capricorn, and rightly so. Who wouldn't want to take practical steps towards ensuring their own success? But plodding through this will not be the answer - it needs a more elegant solution, lighter and more nimble.

Be careful that the
characteristic Capricorn ambition
doesn't tip over into a wider and more
all-encompassing need for control.
Reassure yourself: the unknown is full
of promise, rather than threat.

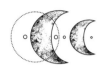

Once in a while, even you can
find yourself overwhelmed Capricorn.
Draw support from those around you
until you feel ready to continue. They
will be pleased and proud that you
trust them to hold you up when
you need it most.

It is important to spend some time in situations that recharge and replenish you Capricorn. Listen to your intuition to understand what you need most right now – whether it be a boost of the spiritual, physical, emotional or intellectual. Or perhaps all of them at once.

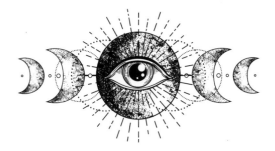

Solving problems is a particular Capricorn strength. But this time you should hold off making a start until you are sure you have the full picture.

You are too sensible to allow much sinking and wallowing Capricorn, but of course there is darkness (much as you try to steer clear of it). Keep something solid under your feet. Welcome the light in, balancing understanding and empathy with the physical activities that bring you joy, to ensure harmony.

It is unusual for details to escape you Capricorn, but once in a while your close-focus means you might fail to grasp the big picture. Take a more relaxed approach to this one and stand back a little further than you usually would so you can survey it properly.

Choose the path that feels
familiar Capricorn. Now is not the time
for branching out in new directions,
but for drawing up that deepest
wisdom to guide you.

No one can truly know your
heart unless you open it to them.
You have many layers Capricorn, and
so much of your true self is hidden
from view. Do not push away those
who seem to instinctively understand
you – they are a gift.

The wise approach this time
is to take the easiest route possible.
Have a look at the ground ahead, there
are plenty of options. Keep a clear
head, and travel light.

When complications begin to
dominate, press pause and disengage,
even just for a short while. A little
careful distance may very well make all
the difference. And remember: 'do
nothing' is always an option.

The more you accept the
irrational, perhaps even the magical,
in your life Capricorn, the more it will
feel as though things are somehow
falling into place... That big, beautiful
jigsaw will start coming together
for you after all.

As a typical Earth sign, you like
to feel stable, grounded and sure
of where you are going Capricorn.
While life is rarely static, you crave
certainty about the way everything is
positioned. Understanding this about
yourself will help you to feel more
in control and confident enough to
adapt when needed.

The constant in life is flux, the
cycle of life and death, movement and
stillness, destruction and creation.
If you struggle against this Capricorn,
you will be fighting a losing battle.
Everything has its time.

You don't really need reminding
of this Capricorn, but since you ask...
Hard work and focus will bring the
success you want, simple as that.

Invest some time into nurturing
those precious relationships Capricorn.
The world doesn't wait, and you can't
expect relationships to flourish and
continue if you don't put in that
essential maintenance along the way.
Don't leave it too late.

You might find it difficult to recognize a good idea if you have had previously negative experiences with the messenger. Do not allow your competitive nature to stand in the way of adopting a solid and sustainable solution. Approach this one with an open mind, and don't neglect to give credit where it is due.

Drawing wisdom from previous experiences does not have to be the same as bearing a grudge, Capricorn. Your memory is long and forgetting is not an option (and neither should it be), but harbouring resentment is not a good investment of your energy. Learn the lesson without holding onto the hurt.

You need clarity and certainty
in order to feel confident Capricorn –
that's just the way you are. If you are
finding yourself second-guessing more
often than you'd like, dig deep and ask
yourself whether this situation
is really working for you.

Bide your time Capricorn;
expending your energies too early
will be a mistake.

Your tough-minded approach often flows through to your treatment of others as well as the criticism-loop you are inclined to play yourself. Ease up.

It can be perplexing to self-sufficient Capricorns, but others often long for your approval and reassurance. Allow them the time and space to feel heard when they want to engage with you; really, they are not asking much. Sometimes just your presence is enough.

Everything can be made to
look good by comparing it with
something worse; context is all when it
comes to making comparisons...
Try to judge this situation
on its own merits.

As a stable Earth sign Capricorn, you draw your strength from reserves of practicality, careful judgement, and the ability to analytically apply your skills where they will be of best use. Inevitably, this means you can easily become intellectually exhausted if you don't pause and replenish along the way. Nurture yourself now.

Even when solitude tugs at
you Capricorn, you still have a slightly
inside-out need to feel that you
belong. Balance respecting your own
needs for separation and quiet while
still maintaining connection
to your support.

You like to surround yourself
with nice things (really, who doesn't?),
but of course you understand that
acquisitions and material wealth carry
no intrinsic value on their own. Focus
instead on enriching your family and
community; such investments will
have far-reaching positive effects
that you can't even begin to
anticipate right now.

Prosperity and wealth should be measured in more than just material possessions; count love, luck and belonging among your blessings Capricorn. Don't focus so determinedly on work that these true treasures slip through your fingers.

Make sure your thinking is done ahead of discussing this issue with other people Capricorn. Voicing your interior monologue before you have reached the point of decision will likely cause confusion and tangled communications.

Usually so self-controlled,
when you occasionally unleash
your anger, sadness or frustration you
can spark a dangerous storm. Deal
with this one step at a time, to avoid
becoming overwhelmed, and at each
stage be mindful of your own
strength and forcefulness. Employ
care and caution, with both
yourself and others.

Adding enjoyment into your daily schedule is sure to bring benefits Capricorn; introducing some playtime will be positive in more ways than one. Consider it a strategy for honing focus and improving output, if that helps.

Do not neglect the truly valuable parts of your life. Commit to restoring perspective and dedicating quality time to the things and people that matter. They will wait for you, but that doesn't mean you should force them to.

Compromising isn't your usual
practice Capricorn – why would
you consider it when you are so often
right? However, on this occasion it
might be the best way to maintain
momentum and avoid stalemate.
Give a little, take a little, then
you can all move on.

There is much you can learn
from the current situation, but
charging straight ahead is not the
way to go. A slower, more considered
approach will help you achieve deeper
understanding and a broader
perspective. You may even be able
to see new opportunities
heading your way.

When you speak from the heart
and ask for what you truly want,
others are sometimes taken by
surprise. Take this as a sign that you
should do it more often, rather than
second-guessing your actions.

Your subconscious has perfected the knack of tapping you on the shoulder every now and again, reminding you of outstanding emotional issues you need to deal with. Remember that this could be about more than just current events... If you are bringing baggage along with you, relieve yourself of the burden now if you can.

Factor in some playtime
Capricorn – all work just won't
cut it. Difficult as you find it to drag
yourself away from your duties,
right now you simply must.

If you know that changes must be made, there's no time like the present to begin; putting them off is simply building up a taller task pile for a later date. It might not be the most enjoyable process, but you will feel a whole lot lighter when it's done.

Once the fun begins, you certainly go with it – and you won't be the first to call it a night. It's just getting you stubborn goats out of the door in the first place that can be difficult, especially when there is so much to do. Make a plan today – an easy, non-complicated, non-work plan – and promise yourself you will see it through.

Don't underestimate the
impact you have on a group Capricorn;
your energy is strong and when your
mood is stormy the thunder
reverberates before you even
say a word. Understand that
you have an effect.

Keeping your leadership vibes
high and bouncing is important right
now; as is so often the case, others
are looking to you to set an
example Capricorn.

Working well with different personalities comes naturally to you Capricorn, but encouraging them all to work together can be a little more of a challenge. Focus on achievable goals and plans that everyone can understand, and a cooperative spirit will naturally arise.

When you have complainers
to deal with, listen and do what you
can Capricorn. But understand as well
that they must also take some
responsibility for their own happiness
– perhaps this just isn't the right
situation for them?

Clearing out and encouraging calm, balance and order (both inside and out) is essential for health and happiness Capricorn. Concentrate on working out what needs to be done and make a determined start.

Are there repairs to be made right now Capricorn, a little list of broken things you keep adding to rather than dealing with? Time to roll up your sleeves and get down to it.

If an unusual (for you) level of dreaminess has been keeping you from more practical matters recently Capricorn, it might be a sign that something on the emotional side is calling for a little more attention.

Stubbornness in others can be a particular frustration, but it often arises from a place of insecurity and self-doubt rather than a desire to be particularly obstinate. Switch on your empathy and compassion when dealing with such issues at the moment.

Be mindful that, in venting your frustrations, you don't negatively impact someone else. You may (briefly) feel relief at finally getting it off your chest, but someone else might feel a whole lot worse.

If you are finding your imagination, or perhaps even your dreams, staying with you during your waking hours, it is time to pay attention. Is there a message your subconscious is trying to send you Capricorn?

When the urge for adventure
takes you, throw caution to the wind.
Time for some fun, goodness knows
you deserve it.

Maintaining your energy and ensuring it is properly channelled and cared for is vital Capricorn – both surges and dips should put you on high alert to pay close attention and adjust your routine. Balancing nourishment, exercise and sleep is especially important when there are so many demands on your time and attention.

Focus on yourself right now Capricorn – there will be time for everything else a little later. Even though all those pressures seem super-urgent, consider the repercussions if you do not first ensure that you are in good coping condition.

Time is a commodity in short supply for you Capricorn, but only because your life is so full of interesting and rewarding things, all of which require investment. Be sure you are using your time wisely, where it will be of greatest benefit to those most important to you.

Your mind's natural agility could do with a boost to ensure you are ready for the challenges the coming days will bring, so be sure you schedule in some downtime and get enough sleep.

Check in with some friends today Capricorn, especially those you have the best times with. Say 'yes' to plans that might be a little out of the ordinary; something unpredictable and wonderful may await.

Angle and delivery are key
to communicative effectiveness
Capricorn. If there is a chance this
will come across as negative, think
carefully before you share
your message.

Quick and capable at the best of times, your patience can be tested by those who are less so. Consider whether there might be a particularly important lesson to learn from their approach Capricorn. Is there something that you could be doing differently (or perhaps even better)?

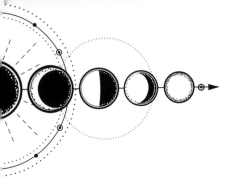

Juggling what looks to others
like too many balls at once is one of
your particular strengths Capricorn.
And while you are more than capable
and often happy to do it, find a way to
make sure others are not taking this
skill of yours for granted.

When you're feeling
indecisive Capricorn, understand
that it may well be the universe's way
of stopping you from making the
wrong decision rather than a
failing on your part.

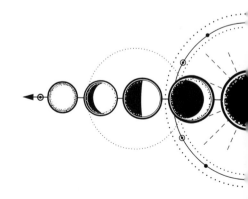

Normally as mentally sure-footed as the mountain goat you are Capricorn, you may have been feeling fuzzy-headed or uncertain of late. Ride it out and wait for the clouds to clear rather than trying to force it.

If you are giving conflicting messages, others may notice and perhaps even complain. It's not like you Capricorn. So, keep quiet and pull back a bit until you feel more certain of yourself and your opinions again.

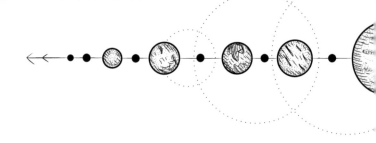

Give more thought than usual
to what you say before you speak
Capricorn. People are listening to you
and will likely act on what you say.
Choose your words carefully.

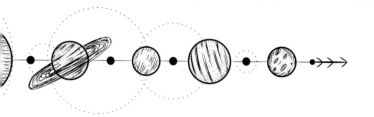

Accept your subconscious desires and intuition rather than pushing them back or rejecting them for not making sense. The more you notice and allow them, without judgement or fear, the better. There is no compulsion to act, but you might find that what you really want enriches your day-to-day life in new and wonderful ways.

Often planned and predictable, you have a spontaneous streak as well, and sometimes it chimes perfectly with the way your energy is flowing. Don't use too much planning or forethought on this one, it will all come together.

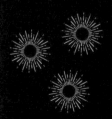

Worry less and plan less, and you will get a lot more done relating to this issue Capricorn. Act on the spur of the moment more often than you usually do, and keep the momentum going. You will find yourself more in tune and in step with those around you.

Spend time around the people you feel you can learn something from Capricorn. Soak up their influence and energy, and don't be afraid to talk to them about what it is you hope to achieve as well. Take inspiration and advice however it arrives.

Processing your feelings and
working on self-improvement is one
thing, but navel-gazing is another.
Don't forget to look up now and again,
give yourself (and those around you)
a break. Step away from all those
emotions and all that self-analysis
for a while.

New ways of thinking will
open up whole new ways of believing,
engaging and understanding.

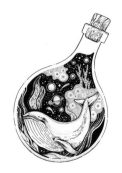

Watch the habits and behaviours of those you admire; it's a good way to learn what makes them tick and to figure out what you might need to adjust to move yourself closer to your own goals.

Disorganization and untidiness in your life are particular problems for you Capricorn, as they raise an alarm about something else going on underneath the surface; some spiritual or emotional turmoil that requires your attention and care. Sorting this out might take some effort. But first, do the dishes and open the post.

Maintaining stamina is dependent on paying attention to your energy levels and what your body and mind need right now Capricorn; you will find yourself in need of focus and endurance over the next little while, if you are going to stay on top form.

Gratification and a sense of pride
in a job you've done well are powerful
Capricorn momentum-drivers.
Pay attention to some small,
easy-to-achieve tasks; completing
them will give you a boost and fire you
up for the bigger things waiting
a little further down the list.

Watch your words right now Capricorn, and think twice, then again, before committing any opinions or judgement to speech or writing. You may not be able to anticipate the impact it could have right now, but any fallout could have a domino effect.

Others can sometimes be
primed to respond in a certain way
before they have even heard what you
have to say – on these occasions you
cannot win, particularly when the
response is emotionally-fuelled. Walk
away from this one Capricorn.

If you are feeling vulnerable,
don't let it stop you exploring. Just
maintain a little distance and keep an
eye on the exits.

Analytical skills are one of your strong points and right now they will come in very handy Capricorn. Weigh everything in the balance and make some cool, clean decisions.

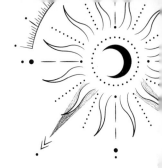

Nurturing relationships with friends and loved ones takes effort Capricorn – is this something you have been neglecting of late? Don't be fooled, the world keeps turning whether or not you notice, and life carries on with or without you. Don't leave it too late. Don't be left behind.

Normally you are such a
cautious sign Capricorn – could it be
you might have been missing
out on something?

Time for some soul-searching,
followed by a heart-to-heart with
those you love Capricorn. Be honest.
Have you let them down? Is there
something you could have done
better? Time to make amends.

Don't spend so much time and effort planning for tomorrow that you forget to make the most of today.

Shifting the focus within your daily routine will be well worth it Capricorn – look at where you could make the day work better for you.

First published in Great Britain in 2021 by
Greenfinch
An imprint of Quercus Editions Ltd
Carmelite House
50 Victoria Embankment
London EC4Y 0DZ

An Hachette UK company

A CIP catalogue record for this book is available
from the British Library

HB ISBN 978-1-52941-237-6

10 9 8 7 6 5 4 3

Designed by Ginny Zeal
Cover design by Andrew Smith
Text by Susan Kelly
All images from Shutterstock.com

Printed and bound in China.

MIX
Paper from
responsible sources
FSC® C016973

Papers used by Greenfinch are from well-managed forests
and other responsible sources.